Contents

Introduction – training aims 2
Basic equipment 3
Diet 5
Fitness determination routine 8
Basic exercises (1) 11
Basic exercises (2) 17
Training routines 23
Leg training 24
Abdominal training 25
Chest training 26
Back training 27
Shoulder training 28
Arm training 29
Stretching 30
Aerobic activity 31
Index 32

Side-lateral raise ▶

Introduction – training aims

Training for strength

Some individuals are naturally stronger than others. Many people make the mistake of thinking that they can train for speed, strength, size and endurance all at the same time. But this is not possible because it is necessary to approach each of these aspects differently to get the required results.

Training for strength involves low repetition work with very heavy weights. The number of repetitions should not exceed 6; even this is high for true strength training. An example of the combination of weight and repetitions would be to use 80% of your maximum lift for 5 reps, followed by 90% of your maximum lift for 3 reps. Whenever all the reps are completed with some strength still in reserve, then the weight should be increased, never the reps.

Pyramid training

Another method of repetition training for strength is to use the pyramid system. Start with 5 reps at 75% of your maximum lift, then increase the weight but decrease the reps to 4. Do this until 1 lift is performed at 90–95% of your maximum and then decrease the weight but increase the reps until you are back to 5 reps at 75% again.

With this system (see table below) 29 reps will be performed, but it is the way they are split up that promotes the development of greater strength. This type of training is very demanding and rest and food intake are most important. At least 1 or 2 rest days will be required between training sessions. Also, you will need to be particularly careful with your diet if you are not to suffer from fatigue. The amount of protein and carbohydrate in the diet will determine how much repair and development can take place, and also how much energy is available to train with.

Training for size

Weight training can produce very different results, depending on the type of routine followed. Even if the majority of exercises employed are basically the same, the results will vary according to whether you work hard for short periods or do easier work for a longer stretch.

When training for size the number of reps per set ranges between 8 and 12. Any less than 8, while developing some strength, would not stimulate muscle growth, and any more than 12 would lead to increased muscular definition but no growth in size. Everybody responds differently to weight training and you must experiment to find the number of reps between 8 and 12 which will promote maximum growth best. You may discover that some muscle groups respond best to 8 reps whereas others, such as the calves or the forearms, respond best to 12 reps. If you find that you are making no gains in size whatso-

Repetitions	5	4	3	2	1	2	3	4	5
Weight	75%	80%	85%	90%	95%	90%	85%	80%	75%

ever, do not be tempted to do more exercises or repetitions because this could lead to overtraining. Instead, try cutting down on the number of exercises, increasing the weight and making sure that you perform 3 sets of at least 8 reps.

Muscles only actually grow after they have recovered from a hard training session. The physical act of training breaks down part of the muscle exercised, and it is during the next 24–72 hours that the muscles recover and begin to grow. Your food intake is of prime importance during the rest and recovery stage. It is no use stimulating muscle growth if your protein intake is insufficient.

There is no quick and easy way to build muscles, but once you obtain the correct balance between training, rest and recovery, and diet, then your muscles certainly will grow.

Training for speed

Muscles are made up of fibres which have different mechanical properties, and two of the main groups of fibres are called fast twitch fibres and slow twitch fibres. The fast twitch fibres have a much higher contraction speed and are associated with dynamic bursts of energy. The slow twitch fibres react much more slowly and are more resistant to fatigue, producing greater endurance. Thus it is clear that you need to work on the fast twitch muscles if you want to improve your speed.

The ratio of fast twitch to slow twitch fibres varies between individuals and is determined by heredity. However, by applying the correct type of training it is possible to make the maximum use of the twitch fibres present. Training for speed must work repeatedly on the fast twitch fibres on a stop–go basis. In the gym the weights must be light and movements explosive; for example you could see how many repetitions you can perform in 10 seconds and then try to beat that amount. Other forms of training might include sprint–stop running or speed skipping.

Training for speed is very taxing and hence you will need to gear your work towards a particular event. Training after a main event should be much less dynamic and should concentrate on improving technique in preparation for the next competition.

Basic equipment

Most people incorrectly believe that you must belong to a gym which is equipped with all the latest equipment in order to make any significant progress in weight training. This is not so. While it is convenient to have lots of equipment at your disposal, it is by no means essential. Excellent gains can be made with the minimum amount of equipment if you are determined.

Three basic pieces of equipment will enable you to perform an enormous variety of exercises to improve your physique or figure. These are the dumbbell/barbell kit, the adjustable bench and the abdominal board.

Dumb-bell/barbell kit

Free weights were used long before machines were invented for weight training, and virtually every exercise can be executed using them. Dumb-bell/barbell kits are inexpensive to buy, and as you become stronger the poundage of the kit can be increased by purchasing additional discs. This way the size of the kit increases gradually with no large cash outlay.

Adjustable bench

Many exercises are performed either sitting or lying across a flat bench. When you also have the option of adjusting the angle of the bench the range of exercises is greatly increased, and it is then possible to develop different parts of muscles much more easily.

An example of this is the basic flat bench press; by performing the bench press with the bench inclined at an angle of 30°, the emphasis of the exercise is placed on the upper pectorals. This would result in muscular development up to the clavicles for a man, preventing a 'droopy' looking chest, while for a woman it would cause a build-up of tissue leading into her cleavage, thus emphasising her bust. If the bench press is done on a decline, the emphasis is placed on the lower pectorals, giving men a strong outline to the lower chest, and women a muscular development which creates the impression of a larger bust.

Abdominal board

Most people need to work their midsections regularly, and having a proper abdominal board encourages this. Sit-ups, crunches, leg raises and knee tucks are all possible on this simple piece of equipment, and as the stomach muscles become stronger the angle of incline is increased so as to bring gravity into play.

Side leg exercises can be done to work the outer thigh area, and a wide variety of scissor-type exercises can be done for the hips and lower stomach areas. (More advanced stomach exercises can be carried out using weights if desired.)

The board can also be used for incline/decline work with barbells and dumb-bells, and does not have to be regarded only as a piece of equipment for exercising the stomach.

It can now be seen that these pieces of equipment constitute a basic gym around which routines for both beginners and advanced trainers can be structured. Whether your aims are physique development or figure improvement, the vast majority of the exercises you will need to do can be carried out with these very basic pieces of equipment.

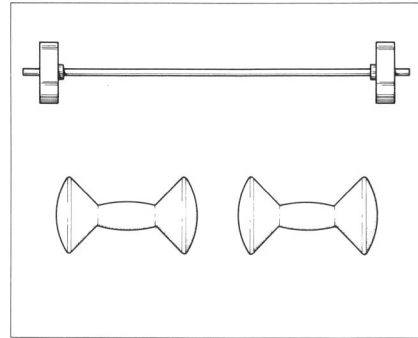

Fig. 1 Dumb-bells and barbell

Abdominal board

Diet

The amount of calories a person needs each day is determined by the type of work they do, the exercise they take and their metabolic rate. It is very simple to work out the amount of calories needed each day. For 7 days count the calories in every piece of food you eat and every drink you consume. Add these amounts together and then divide the total by 7. This will give you your average daily calorie intake. If your weight remains constant you must be using up all your calories, but if you are gaining weight then some of the calories you consume are being stored as fat. If you are losing weight, then you are not consuming sufficient calories daily. Once you know your daily calorie intake it is easy to adjust it so that you gain or lose weight.

When exercise is concentrated on specific areas it will help to tone up the muscles faster and so tighten the skin, giving the impression of increased weight loss in the desired areas. It is the distribution of a person's body-weight that is most important. Since muscle is heavier than fat but not as bulky, a small increase in muscle size compensates for a larger amount of fat loss, resulting in a considerable change in shape but no change in body-weight.

Protein

Training breaks down muscle tissue and during rest periods the tissue is repaired and growth takes place if sufficient protein is available. So how much protein do you need? The most widely accepted figure is 0.6g (0.02oz) per pound of body-weight. Thus a person weighing 154lb (70kg) would need 154 x 0.6 = 92.4g (3.23oz) per day. This amount would maintain the person's health and keep his weight steady; to promote growth an extra 10–15g (0.35–0.5oz) per day would be necessary. Excessive protein intake can be dangerous, putting stress on the kidneys and causing dehydration.

The protein content of food varies considerably, and the following are average values for some of the better sources. (Remember that these values will depend upon the size of the egg, the type of milk, the cut of the steak and so on.)

Egg (1)	6g (0.2oz)
Milk (pint)	12g (0.4oz)
Cheese (28g or 1oz)	6g (0.2oz)
Chicken (28g or 1oz)	7g (0.24oz)
Fish (28g or 1oz)	5g (0.17oz)
Steak (28g or 1oz)	5g (0.17oz)

It is perfectly possible to obtain all the protein you need from a balanced daily diet. However, the protein must be eaten in amounts not exceeding 20–25g (0.7–0.88oz) at a time because the body is unable to digest more than this and any extra will just pass through the body. This is why people who want to build muscle have 4 or 5 smaller meals throughout the day. Since this is not suitable for everyone, protein drinks are a convenient alternative.

Carbohydrates

There are two types of carbohydrates; simple and complex. The basic difference is that simple carbohydrates are refined complex carbohydrates, so that if you remove the nutrients from the complex carbohydrates you end up with simple ones. Hence complex carbohydrates are better for bodybuilders and athletes.

Complex carbohydrates are found in cereals, fruit and vegetables, while simple carbohydrates are found in white bread, white flour and any food containing white sugar. Sugar is positively detrimental to bodybuilding due to the fact that it causes a rise in insulin levels. Intensive training routines cause the release of growth hormone from the pituitary gland, but insulin can block the release of this hormone and thereby nullify the effects of training.

The source of energy for a muscle contraction is Adenosine Triphosphate (A.T.P.) and this occurs in very small amounts in human muscle. Therefore, it needs to be rapidly regenerated if exercise is to continue, and this regeneration is brought about by a substance called Creatine Phosphate (C.P.). The splitting of the A.T.P. and C.P. molecules is the prime source of muscular energy. These processes are anaerobic (without oxygen) and no lactic acid is formed in the muscles. The length of time for these processes to occur is very short (up to 6 seconds). After this the energy is supplied by the breakdown of muscle glycogen into lactic acid. Glycogen is produced from complex carbohydrate, and therefore the energy required for training is ultimately derived from the complex carbohydrates you eat. It is possible to break down fat to use as energy when you are training, but it is essentially glycogen which is the energy source.

In order to ensure that enough glycogen is present for training, carbohydrates should make up approximately half of your daily diet. It is also advisable to take a vitamin B supplement to aid in the digestion of the carbohydrate.

Once the carbohydrate has been consumed it is stored as glycogen in the muscles and stays there until it is required for energy. This storage of glycogen in the muscles adds to the overall size of the muscles. Once training is underway the glycogen is gradually removed from the muscles to produce energy and is replaced by blood, that is the muscles are 'pumped'. After training has finished the blood supply is reduced and the 'pump' disappears, resulting in the muscle being smaller than before the exercise started. A fresh source of glycogen is then needed to restore the muscles to their original size and to encourage growth of the muscle tissue. Therefore, complex carbohydrates are initially more important after a work-out that protein.

Complex carbohydrates are best taken regularly throughout the day so that the glycogen is steadily replaced and built up in the muscles. Lack of complex carbohydrates in the daily diet is very often the cause of sportspeople feeling under par.

Iron

Iron has a crucial role to play in the efficient working of the human body and is vital to healthy living. The main function of iron is to form the red pigment in the blood called haemoglobin. (Up to 80% of the iron in the body is used daily in this way, with approximately 20% being stored mainly in the liver and the bone marrow.) When not enough iron is available the amount of haemoglobin in the blood is reduced, leading to a decrease in the amount of oxygen which can be transported from the lungs to the tissues. The effects of this decrease in oxygen transportation are tiredness, lack of stamina, a pale complexion and the inside of the eyelid becoming colourless. If the iron deficiency is not remedied the organs of the body may be affected, and when all of these factors are combined the results can be severe, with the person suffering from headaches, insomnia, dizziness, loss of appetite, shortness of breath and reduced resistance to infection.

A well balanced diet will provide enough iron for the average person, but sportspeople may need to supplement their diet with 15–20g (0.5–0.7oz) of iron per day. You should not exceed this amount because iron can be toxic in certain individuals. One of the best forms of supplement is haemoglobin iron which is derived from beef blood and is completely natural (virtually 100% of it is used by the body compared to very low utilisation by the body of synthetic iron–ferrous salts). Haemoglobin iron can be taken on its own or with desiccated liver. Eggs and ordinary liver are the best sources of iron in food.

Desiccated liver

This is perhaps one of the most widely used and cheapest of supplements in bodybuilding. It is produced from raw beef liver, and once in its dried form is one of the most concentrated forms of food available. It has all the goodness of liver but with virtually all the moisture, fibre and fat taken out. Desiccated liver is approximately 80% protein and is easily broken down and absorbed by the stomach. It contains all the essential amino acids and all the known B vitamins, but perhaps its most important constituent is haemoglobin iron.

If you are only going to take one form of supplement then desiccated liver should be your choice.

Basic vitamins – vitamin B complex and vitamin C

When the majority of athletes begin to take vitamin supplements the most basic mistake they make is to take too many without considering which is going to help them most. The type of vitamin taken should depend on the general state of health of the individual and the type of diet he follows.

Vitamin B

The 'B' vitamins are a very complex group, with each individual 'B' vitamin contributing to a different aspect of fitness. However, a general consideration of the 'B' group is of great importance to both the serious and the casual trainer. The vitamin B complex enables the body to make full use of the food consumed. Part of the group helps in the use of carbohydrate for energy and growth (B_1 thiamin), while vitamin B_6 (pyridoxine) helps in using protein and fats and also in removing water from the body tissues (diuretic). Niacin aids blood circulation, which means that protein is carried to the muscles more efficiently, and also helps muscle recovery by carrying waste products away more quickly. Pantothenic acid is important in the digestion of protein. Choline and inositol help to break down fat. Vitamin B_{12} helps to produce red blood cells which carry oxygen, and therefore prevents anaemia and tiredness. Vitamin B_{15} (pangamic acid) helps the muscles to retain oxygen, thus combatting fatigue.

The 'B' complex can be obtained by taking desiccated liver and yeast tablets, or by taking a special 'B' complex capsule. The result is better utilisation of the food being eaten, accompanied by a feeling of well-being and more drive during training.

Vitamin C

The body cannot store vitamin C so it is essential to have a fresh supply every day. Since vitamin C is water soluble any excess is excreted and so you don't have to worry about taking too much. Vitamin C helps to combat stress either from worry or from intense physical exercise. Therefore the amount taken needs to be related to the type of job a person has and also the type of training he undertakes. Athletes in combat sports should take large amounts of vitamin C to help combat bruising and soreness. Marathon runners need large amounts to help combat the stresses experienced in the ankles, the knees and the hips. Bodybuilders can obtain relief from vitamin C for the aches and pains they suffer in the shoulders and elbows.

Vitamin C is readily available in citrus fruits and green peppers. Alternatively, it can be taken in tablet or capsule form. If the latter option is taken, it is better to spread the intake throughout the day so as to continually top up the body's supply. The recommended amount to take varies, but usually ranges between 1–6g (0.03–0.2oz) per day. A person will soon know if he has exceeded his body's tolerance because excess vitamin C produces the 'runs'.

Fitness determination routine

This routine is designed to increase a person's pulse rate, and then to monitor its decrease over a set period of time. The rate of decrease of the pulse after vigorous exercise is a good indication of the overall fitness of an individual. The routine should not be attempted by anyone with a heart condition or high blood pressure. If you have any doubts about your present health, you must consult your doctor beforehand.

The only equipment you need is a watch or a clock with a second hand or second display. The 3 easiest places to take your pulse are the wrist, the side of the neck and the temples. To take your pulse all you need to do is to count it for 10 seconds and then multiply by 6. This will give your pulse rate per minute.

At the start of the routine, when you are in a relaxed state, you take your pulse and note the reading (reading 1).

At the end of the very last exercise you immediately take your pulse again and note the reading (reading 2). You then wait, standing still for 1 minute, and take a final pulse reading (reading 3). Subtract the third reading from the second, which will generally give you a value between 0 and 50. This is the value which indicates your fitness.

0–10	poor
10–20	fair
20–30	average
30–40	good
40–50	very good
50+	excellent

Your pulse rate will continue to decrease until it reverts to the first reading. The time taken to revert to the relaxed state is directly related to the fitness of the body. Each exercise only lasts 15 seconds, and in that time you must complete as many repetitions as possible. You then have 15 seconds' rest, during which time you must stand still. As soon as the 15 seconds' rest has elapsed, you must start the next exercise. The total time of the exercises from start to finish is 3 minutes 45 seconds.

The exercises are detailed below; it is advisable to practise each exercise individually before attempting the whole routine.

Touch toes

Start off by standing upright with the arms above your head. Bend from the waist, with your arms still straight, and touch your toes. Return to the start position and repeat.

Press-ups

Lie face down on the floor with your feet together and your hands shoulder width apart. Keeping the body rigid, press with the hands until the arms are straight. Lower your body to the floor but do not touch it, and repeat. (Anyone having difficulties may leave the hips and legs rest on the floor until strength increases.)

Running on the spot

The knees must come up as fast as possible to waist height.

Sit-ups

Lie on your back with your knees bent. Put your hands over your ears and sit up until your elbows touch your knees. Return to the lying position and repeat. (You may hook your toes under a chair if you like, but do not link your fingers behind your head as this puts strain on your neck.)

Knees up to chest

Stand upright and do high jumps, bringing both knees up to the chest at the same time. Do not crouch to the floor.

Squat thrusts

Start from a crouched position with your hands touching the floor at either side of your feet. Kick your legs back approximately 0.6m (2ft), supporting your body with straight arms. As soon as your feet touch the floor behind you, spring back to the starting position and repeat.

High jumps

Start from a crouched position and jump as high into the air as possible with your arms above your head. Repeat.

Star jumps

Stand upright with your arms by your sides. Jump to a position with your legs apart and your arms in a 'ten to two' position. Return to the start and repeat.

Advanced use of the fitness determination routine (FDR)

By now you should be completely familiar with the original FDR, and you will already have experienced its benefits. It might already have occurred to you that the routine can be varied to produce different benefits. The object of advanced use of the FDR is to make you aware of its potential.

The first and most obvious change is to increase the duration of each exercise, but keeping the rest periods constant, that is 30 seconds' exercise followed by 15 seconds' rest. This relatively small increase causes much more work for the heart and lungs, and will result in greater cardio-vascular fitness. Once this increase becomes easier, change to 45 seconds' exercise followed by 15 seconds' rest. Again the results will be dramatic. It should be stressed that these increases should not be attempted unless you are finding the original routine fairly easy.

A second possible change is to swap one exercise for another, for example sit-ups for crunches. Once a routine becomes boring it is soon forgotten and its benefits are lost. If you feel the exercises are not hard enough for you, substitute more difficult ones. When doing this, try to keep a balance between upper and lower body exercises. For people who are training for a particular sport such as karate, specific exercises can be inserted in the routine, for example alternate mae-geri or squat/stand-up/mae-geri. The variations are virtually endless and are only limited by the imagination of the individual.

A third change, and probably the most physically demanding, is to introduce weights into the routine. The routine then becomes very specific and is no longer a general fitness method of training. With weights, the routine can be used to greatly increase the muscular endurance of the legs and the stomach muscles. The use of weights coupled with longer exercise periods is very demanding and is only intended for serious athletes.

The Fitness Determination Routine must be used to enhance your existing training, not to compete with it. Therefore, if you are in a building-up period as far as weight training is concerned, you should keep the FDR work at a low rate. That way you will not burn off too many calories which might prevent you from increasing muscle size. Conversely, if you are building up to a competition and wish to greatly increase your fitness and endurance, the FDR should be very intense and should make up a large part of your training. This also applies to bodybuilders who need to reduce body fat. The harder and faster they work, the more calories they will burn up and the leaner they will become.

Finally, it must be stressed that increases or changes in the rate of work should only be carried out once a person has attained a high standard of physical fitness. If you have not used the FDR regularly over the past six months, do not change it.

Basic exercises (1)

The following section deals with the basic exercises you will use during the first 6 months. These exercises will be used on your first 3 routines, and will be incorporated in stages so as to make your training progressive and more demanding. It is necessary to follow the routines exactly to obtain the best results.

Style is very important, and it is important to execute the movement slowly and strictly. Refer to the available photographs when reading the exercise description, and practise them on their own first before attempting a whole session.

Remember that a full set of weights is not essential for the routines. House bricks can be used instead of dumb-bells and a plank on bricks can be used instead of a bench. Similarly, a wooden bar with a box on either end will serve as a barbell and this can easily be weighted by filling the boxes with soil or sand.

Sit-ups
(see p.9)

Twists
Standing upright, hold a stick horizontally at the back of your neck. Twist your body to the left as far as possible, and then round to the right as far as possible. This counts as one movement. Keep your feet and hips still and keep facing forwards. Hold your stomach in during the twists.

Knee raise
Lie on your back with your hands over your ears and your legs out straight. Raise your left knee as far as possible, and raise your right elbow to meet it. Return to the flat position then raise your right knee as far as possible, and raise your left elbow to meet it. This counts as one movement.

Bench press
Lie flat on the bench. Grip the bar with the hands shoulder width apart and the arms straight up. Lower the bar slowly to the top of the chest, touching the chest lightly with the bar and pressing until the arms are straight. Do not let the weight drop to the chest and never 'bounce' the bar off the chest. This exercise is best done with a partner to assist. An alternative exercise is wide press-ups with the hands on house bricks (these will allow a greater stretch).

Dumb-bell flyes
Lie flat on the bench with the dumb-bells held out above your chest. Bend the elbows slightly. Slowly lower the elbows apart until a full stretch is obtained. Pull evenly back to the vertical position, concentrating on the chest muscles all the time.

Pull-over
Lie across the bench with the dumb-bell overhead and the elbows slightly bent. Slowly lower the dumb-bell as far behind the head as possible, keeping the hips down. Inhale as you stretch. Pull the dumb-bell slowly back to the overhead position, then breathe out.

Side-lateral raise
Stand upright with the dumb-bells by your sides. Slowly raise your arms out to the sides until they are horizontal. Lower them again slowly.

Dumb-bell shoulder press – slowly press the dumb-bells vertically until the arms are straight

Dumb-bell shoulder press

Stand upright with the arms bent and the dumb-bells at shoulder height. Slowly press vertically until the arms are straight. Lower them slowly to shoulder height. Do not twist the dumb-bells during the press.

Bent-over lateral raise

Bend from the waist until the torso is horizontal, and the arms are hanging straight below. Slowly raise the arms apart until they are horizontal (keep the elbows slightly bent). Lower them slowly to the start position.

Squats

Stand upright with the feet approximately 46cm (18in) apart and pointing out slightly. Hold the bar across your shoulders at the back of the neck. Bend the knees until the thighs are parallel to the floor, keeping the head up. Do not bend forwards. Push slowly to the upright position. The knees should be pointing at the same angle as the toes. This exercise is best done with a partner for safety and assistance if necessary.

An alternative exercise is the one-

Squats – bend the knees until the thighs are parallel to the floor

Lunges

legged squat. Stand upright on one leg, keeping the other leg straight out in front. Bend your supporting leg until the thigh is parallel to the floor and then push until the leg is straight again. The other leg must remain straight out all the time, and must not touch the floor. Complete all reps on one leg and then change over. You may hold the wall to help your balance.

Calf raise

The starting position is the same as for the squat. Raise up slowly on to your toes, as high as possible, keeping your body upright. Do not lean forwards. Lower yourself slowly. You may place a 5cm (2in) thick block of wood under the balls of your feet to make the exercise harder.

Hold the bar across the shoulders behind the head. Stand with your right leg about 60cm (2ft) in front of your left one, and slowly lower your body forwards until your right thigh is parallel to the floor. Keep your back straight and vertical. Your left leg should be bent and should nearly touch the floor. Slowly push upwards with your right leg until it is almost straight. Repeat all movements on 1 leg without straightening it. Change to the left leg and repeat.

Upright rowing

Stand upright holding the barbell in front of you, with your arms straight down, palms facing the body and hands approximately 15cm (6in) apart. Slowly pull the barbell upwards, keeping it close to the stomach and chest until it is just underneath the chin and the elbows are pointing upwards. Lower slowly to the start position. Do not bend the back and do not sway.

Bent-over rowing

Bend from the waist until the torso is horizontal, the arms are hanging out straight below, and you holding the barbell with hands shoulder width apart. Slowly pull up the bar until it touches the chest, and then slowly lower it to arm's length. Stretching and contraction should be felt in the back, but do not rock or jerk.

Hyperextensions

Lie face down on the floor with your hands touching in the small of the back and your legs straight out and together. Slowly arch the back and lift the chest and head upwards and back. At the same time raise the feet off the floor as

Upright rowing – slowly pull the barbell upwards until just underneath the chin

Bent-over rowing – slowly pull up the bar until it touches the chest

far as possible. Hold this position for 2 seconds, then slowly lower them to the floor.

Triceps extension

Stand upright with the left hand on the hip. The right hand should hold the dumb-bell straight overhead. Slowly lower the dumb-bell to the back of the head, keeping the upper arm vertical. Press slowly to the vertical position.

Triceps kickback

Bend from the waist until the torso is horizontal. Hold the dumb-bell in the right hand. Keep the upper arm horizontal, with the forearm and dumb-bell hanging straight down. Slowly straighten the arm by lifting the dumb-bell backwards, keeping the upper arm still. The palm of the hand should now be facing the floor. Slowly lower the forearm to the starting position. The left arm can either hold the wall or a knee to assist balance.

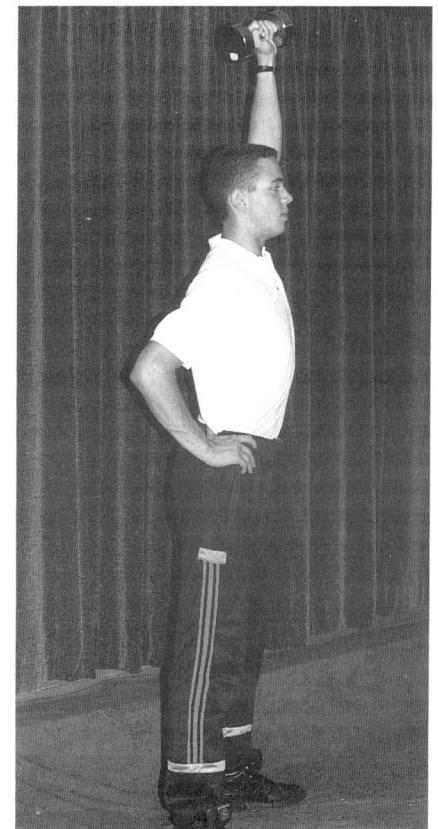

Triceps extension – slowly lower the dumb-bell to the back of the head and then press to the vertical position

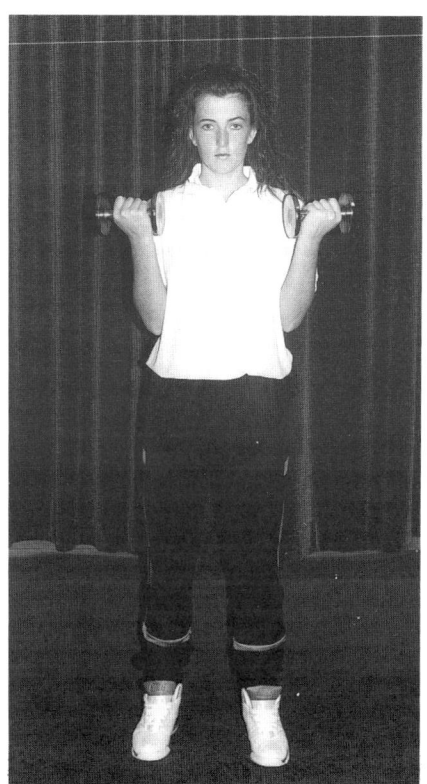

Dumb-bell curls – curl the dumb-bells upwards to shoulder height

Dumb-bell curls

Stand upright, with your arms holding the dumb-bells by your sides and your palms facing inwards. Slowly curl the dumb-bells upwards to shoulder height, twisting them gradually during the full movement until the palms are facing you. Slowly lower the dumb-bells to the start position. Do not arch the back during the exercise, and do not swing the dumb-bells.

Barbell curl

Stand upright with the arms straight down, holding the barbell with the hands shoulder width apart and the palms facing outwards. Slowly curl the barbell to shoulder height, and then lower it slowly to the starting position. Do not lean backwards or jerk the barbell upwards as this will put great strain on the lower back area and detract from the development of the biceps.

Basic exercises (2)

This section deals with the basic exercises that will be incorporated into the more advanced training routines outlined later. They are designed to work the various muscle groups from slightly different angles, and will enable you to vary your routines according to your requirements.

Once again the importance of style needs to be stressed, given that the poundage you lift does not matter as much as the way in which you lift it.

Wrist curl

Sit on the end of a bench, holding the barbell with hands 15cm (6in) apart. Bend forwards and rest your forearms on the bench with your hands hanging over the edge. Slowly let your fingers unfurl and let the barbell roll down to your fingertips. Now slowly curl your fingers upwards, gripping the barbell, and curl your wrists as high as possible without lifting your forearms off the bench. Repeat the exercise. This exercise must be done slowly and carefully so as not to let the barbell drop from your fingertips.

Crunches

Lie on your back, with your hands over your ears, your knees bent and your ankles crossed. Slowly 'crunch' your head and knees together and then lower your head back on to the floor. The knees should only move slightly – it is the head and upper body movement towards the knees which produces the best results.

◀ Barbell curl – slowly curl the barbell to shoulder height, then lower it to the starting position

Leg raises

Lie flat with your legs completely off the bench. Keeping the legs straight, raise them until they are almost vertical and then lower them until they are almost touching the floor. Keep your lower back flat against the bench to prevent any strain. This exercise can be done lying flat on the floor, but using a bench stretches the lower abdomen more.

Flat dumb-bell press

Lie flat on the bench with your arms out straight holding the dumb-bells and your palms facing your feet. Make sure that the dumb-bell bars are lower than the top of your chest. Slowly press out until your arms are straightened again and your palms are facing down as before.

Incline dumb-bell flyes

Set the bench at an angle of 30–45°. Lie on the bench with arms out straight, almost vertical, and hold the dumb-bells with palms facing each other. Slowly lower the arms, still keeping them slightly bent at the elbows until the dumb-bells are level with the chest. Slowly raise until vertical, breathing

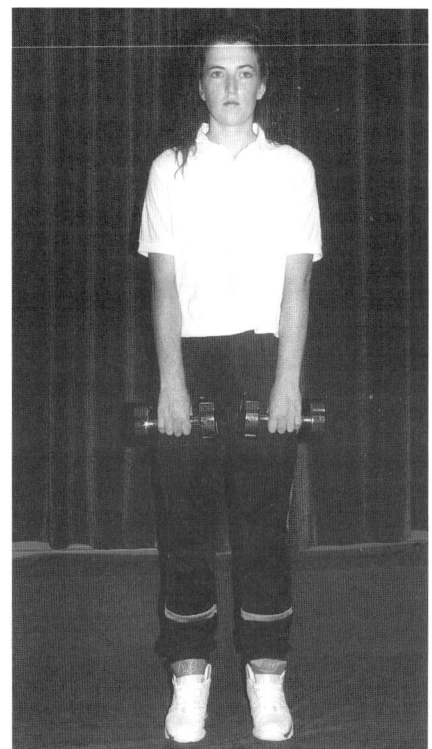 

Front dumb-bell raise – alternately raise each arm outwards in front until horizontal and then slowly lower

out. This exercise develops the upper chest and the front deltoid.

Front dumb-bell raise

Stand upright with the dumb-bells on the front of the thighs and the palms facing the thighs. Alternately raise each arm outwards in front of you until horizontal and then slowly lower, keeping the arms straight at all times. The emphasis here is on developing the front deltoid – excellent for martial artists.

Barbell press

Stand upright, holding the bar at shoulder height in front of your chest with your palms facing outwards. Slowly press upwards until your arms are straight overhead, then lower gradually to the top of the chest again. Do not arch the back and do not jerk.

Dead lift

Squat down with your feet just over shoulder width apart. Hold the bar with an alternate grip, that is one palm facing outwards and one facing inwards. The back must be straight or slightly arched, never rounded. Gradually straighten the legs until you are standing upright, then lower slowly to the floor without jerking. It is advisable to wear a weight-training belt for this exercise because of the strain on the lower back. Do not use this exercise if you have lower back problems.

▲ Barbell press – press upwards until the arms are straight overhead ▶

Seated calf raise

Sit on the edge of the bench, with the balls of the feet on a 15cm (6in) block of wood. Place the barbell across your knees, holding it in place with your hands. Slowly lower your heels to the floor, gaining full stretch. Next, raise the heels until they are as high as possible without moving the balls of the feet. Hold the contraction for 2 seconds, then lower again.

One-arm dumb-bell rowing

Place one knee and one hand on the bench for balance. Bend over, holding the heavy dumb-bell below the bench. Slowly raise the dumb-bell vertically as high as possible without jerking or rocking, keeping it close to the body. The elbow should be high. Complete the set on one arm and then change sides.

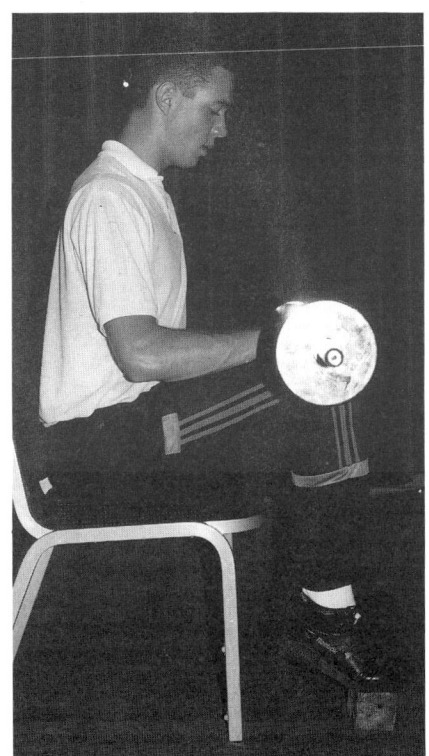

Seated calf raise – raise the heels as high as possible without moving the balls of the feet

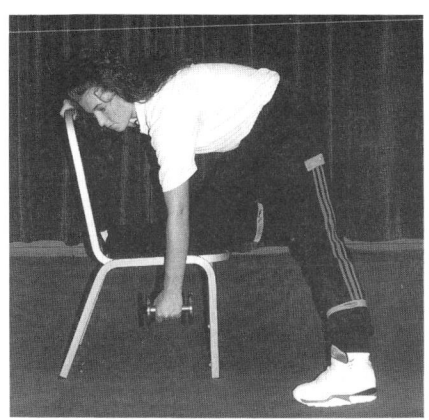

One-arm dumb-bell rowing – slowly raise the dumb-bell without jerking or rocking, keeping it close to the body ▶

Stiff-legged dead lift

Stand upright, holding the barbell in front of your thighs. Slowly bend from the waist, lowering the bar towards the floor and keeping the legs straight. Lower as far as possible without bending the legs and then gradually stand up straight again. This exercise must be done slowly with no jerking movements. It exercises the lower back and stretches the hamstrings.

Triceps dips

This exercise can be executed using 2 benches or 2 chairs. Hold on to the edge of 1 bench with your hands behind your back. Put your heels on the other bench with your legs out straight. Slowly bend your arms, lowering the upper body towards the floor and keeping the legs straight until the elbows form right angles, then slowly straighten up. The exercise can be made more difficult by placing a weight across the thighs.

Triceps dips – lower the upper body until the elbows form right angles ▶

Close grip bench press

Lie flat on the bench, holding the barbell with your hands 15–23cm (6–9in) apart. Slowly lower and touch your chest with the bar. Then press upwards until the arms are locked straight out and the triceps are fully contracted. Close hand press-ups also have the same effect.

Swing-bell curls

A 46cm (18in) centre-loaded bar is used in this exercise. Sit on the edge of the bench with your knees apart. Bend over, holding the ends of the bar at arm's length. Slowly curl until the weights touch your chest, staying bent over the weight all the time.

Concentration curls

Sit on the edge of the bench with your knees apart. Bend over, holding the dumb-bell at arm's length between your knees, with the back of your elbow pressing against the inside of the thigh. Slowly curl until the dumb-bell touches your shoulder. Do not jerk or swing. Complete a set on 1 arm and then change arms.

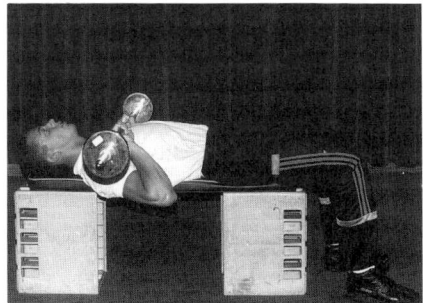

Close grip bench press – slowly lower and touch your chest with the bar, then press upwards until the arms are locked straight out

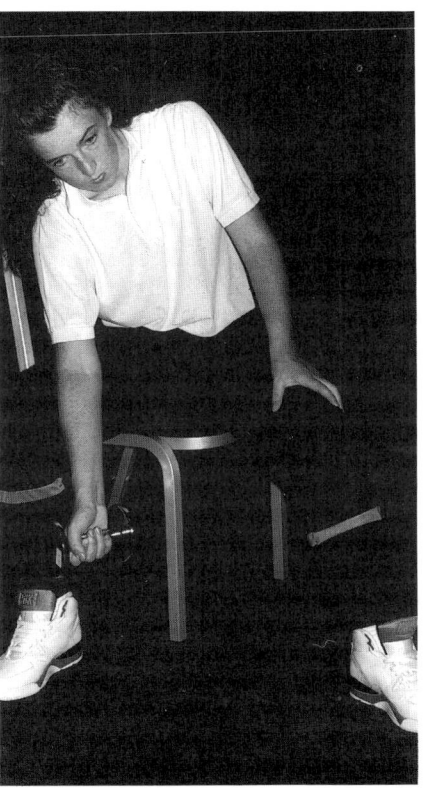

▲ Concentration curls – slowly curl until the dumb-bell touches the shoulder ▶

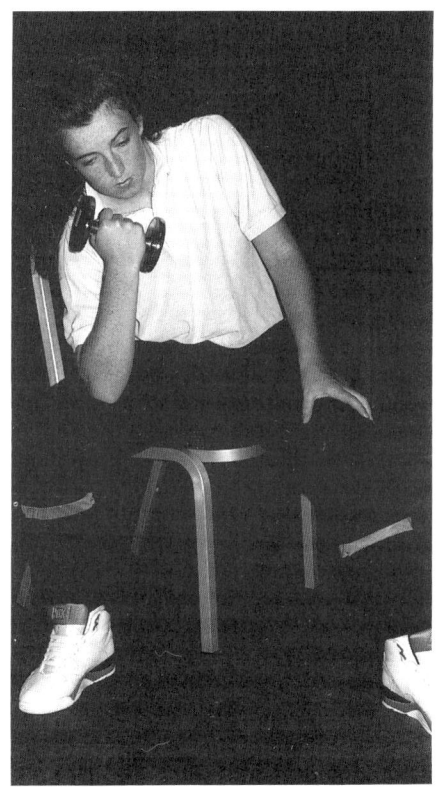

Training routines

The following 6 routines are designed to last 8 weeks each and they become progressively harder. Do not be tempted to start a harder routine at the beginning as this will almost certainly detract from the potential gains.

Each training session should begin with 5 minutes' stretching, 5 minutes' skipping and a 15-second circuit of the fitness determination routine (see page 8). This warm-up period will take less than 15 minutes to complete, but will increase cardio-vascular fitness and ensure that the muscles are ready for action. Remember, the majority of muscle strains and pulls are the result of insufficient warming up.

All of the routines are designed for complete body training 3 times a week. Always have a day's rest between training; growth only takes place after the muscles have fully recovered from the previous training session, generally after 48 hours.

Sets and repetitions

Routine 1
1st session	1 set of 10 repetitions for each exercise
2nd session	2 sets of 10 repetitions for each exercise
3rd session	3 sets of 10 repetitions for each exercise

This gradual build-up of reps over the first 3 sessions will reduce the amount of stiffness and soreness experienced in the muscles at the start of the programme. Thereafter 3 sets of 10 repetitions should be used for most exercises in all routines. The exceptions to this include the abdominals, the calves and the forearms. You can increase the abdominal repetitions to any number you like as long as 3 sets are performed. Repetitions for calves and forearms can be increased to sets of 15 because they are composed of denser, more resilient muscle fibres and the need to be worked harder.

The weights used should be increased once 3 sets of 10 repetitions have been achieved so as to make the weight training progressive.

The routine sheets should be filled in each week or whenever the weight is increased. After a few sessions you will know which weights to use, but you should make sure that the routine is kept up to date. It is good psychologically to look back and see just how much you have improved both in terms of strength and physique. This should provide you with the incentive to train harder and achieve even more.

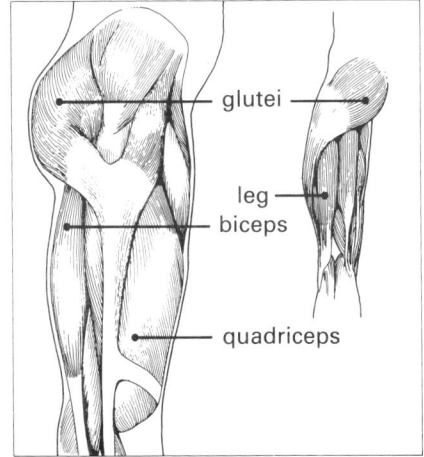

Fig. 2 Upper leg muscles

Leg training

All too often leg training is neglected, resulting in a lack of balance between the legs and the upper body. However, the problem is more predominant in men; women tend to spend around two thirds of their training time working on their legs and glutei (buttocks).

Well-equipped gyms will have a large selection of leg machines designed to isolate the various muscle groups. But there will never be an exercise as good as squats for working all of the muscles together. Correct squatting works the quadriceps, the leg biceps, the calves and the glutei and also gives the heart and lungs a good work-out. Squatting is an anabolic exercise in that it promotes growth in all other muscle groups as well as specialising on the legs.

The front of the thigh is composed of four muscles which are collectively known as the quadriceps. These are responsible for straightening, lifting and rotating the leg. The back of the leg has large muscles known as the leg biceps which bend the leg. The calve muscles at the back of the shin bone make it possible to raise the heel. The gluteus maximus muscle in the buttocks makes it possible to pull the legs back, push the hips forward and stand up straight.

Beginners and intermediate trainers rarely need to do more than squats or calf raises to achieve good leg development. If these are done with moderate weights in strict style during the early stages of training, then very good foundations will have been laid for more advanced, specialised exercises. Lunges will place more emphasis on the quadriceps and glutei, and are therefore excellent for women to raise sagging bottoms. Front squats also place more emphasis on the quadriceps.

The calves can be trained in isolation by using seated calf raises or standing calf raises. The former works the soleus (lower) muscle more, while the latter works the gastrocnemius (upper) muscle. Remember that an over-developed soleus will give the appearance of a 'thick' ankle, so aim for balance between the two rather than just increased size.

The most effective way of isolating the leg biceps is by using a hamstring machine to perform leg curls. Without this machine the best method is to do dead lifts; the negative part of this exercise (resistance to dropping) really works the leg biceps very hard.

The glutei are worked in squats, lunges and dead lifts, but one other very simple exercise is straight leg kicks to the rear. These can be done free standing, with ankle weights or strapped to a pulley machine.

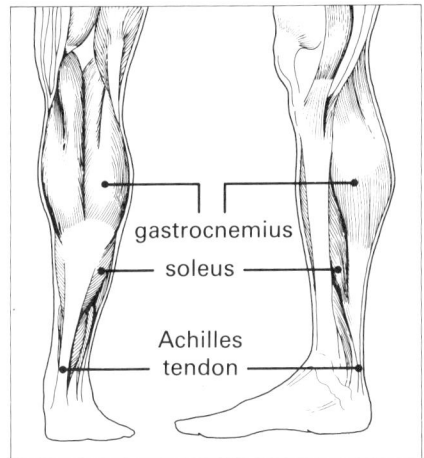

Fig. 3 Lower leg muscles

Abdominal training

The abdominals are perhaps the most striking and impressive of all the muscle groups. The waistline is usually the first area where fat accumulates, and so the presence of well developed and well defined abdominals is an obvious sign of an excellent physical state.

The stomach muscles are made up of several muscle groups, the most important being the rectus abdominis and the external oblique. The rectus abdominis is a large flat muscle which joins the sternum (breast bone) to the pubic bone. This is divided vertically by the linea alba, and horizontally by 3 fibrous bands. These fibrous bands create the impressive 'washboard' look of the abdominals. The external obliques are situated either side of the rectus abdominis, and run diagonally from top to bottom. It is the obliques and abdominals which create the well trained look.

Thus because there are stomach muscles which operate vertically, diagonally and horizontally, complex bending and twisting movements are possible, and support for the vital abdominal organs is provided.

One of the most popular myths in weight training is that higher reps produce bigger abdominals. However, in order for the abdominals to grow you must treat them like any other muscle group, and work them hard for 8 to 12 reps using 3 to 4 sets.

Two of the most basic exercises for increasing abdominal development are weighted sit-ups and weighted leg raises. To do these effectively you need either an abdominal board which can be used on an incline, or a plank with one end raised on bricks and a piece of rope tied to that end to hook your feet underneath. (The angle of the incline board can be made steeper as strength and fitness increases.)

For the sit-ups either a dumb-bell or a weight disc is held to the chest, and the back is kept slightly rounded with the chin on the chest. The start and finish positions are such that there is no rest until all the reps have been completed. The sit-ups start with the back off the board, and end before the upper body reaches the vertical position. When you lower to the start position, do not touch the board; if you do this, or if you sit up past the vertical position, then the abdominals will have a slight rest.

The leg raises are done the opposite way round, with the feet at the lower end of the incline bench. Either iron boots or weights are strapped to the ankles and the legs are raised to an almost vertical position. The legs are then lowered to within 15cm (6in) of the bench before being raised again. Try not to arch the back during this exercise.

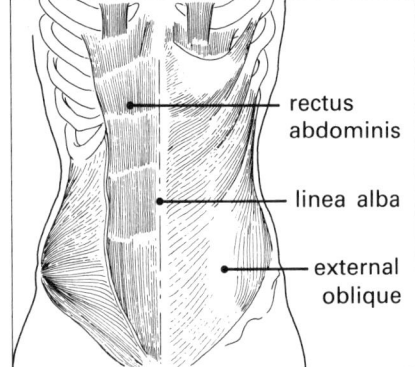

Fig. 4 Abdominal muscles

Chest training

Good chest development is generally accepted as an indication of strength. The link between strength and chest development is probably due to the fact that bench pressing is the prime chest builder and is now one of the most basic of all bodybuilding exercises. The chest muscles are called the pectoralis major and pectoralis minor – 'pecs' for short. The pectoralis minor lies underneath the pectoralis major and in almost all cases any reference to the pecs means the pectoralis major.

The pecs respond fairly quickly to regular training, especially the flat bench press. The main function of the pecs is to adduct the arms (adduction is a movement towards the centre-line of the body), that is they move the upper arms across the body as in dumb-bell flyes. Other movements brought about by the pecs are shoulder flexion, which draws the arm forwards and upwards, and shoulder extension, which draws the arm down and forwards. By working the pecs from different angles it is possible to direct the work-load to different parts of the muscle.

To develop the pecs fully it is necessary to be aware of how much development there is already, and whether that development is well balanced. The most common problem for men is to develop too much lower pectoral muscle, and so end up with a 'droopy' looking chest. Conversely, too much upper pectoral development and too little lower pectoral development gives the impression of a chest that 'fades' away. Both of these common faults can easily be rectified by using the correct exercises.

The range of chest exercises is really only limited by the equipment that is available. The flat bench press is very good for building size, and fairly heavy poundages can be used quite quickly. Varying the grip on the barbell alters the range of movement but too wide a grip reduces the range of movement, leading to restricted development. Bench pressing should never be done alone because of the dangers of getting the barbell stuck across the face, neck or chest.

There are two variations on the bench press – the incline bench press and the decline bench press. The incline bench press puts more emphasis on upper pec development and the decline bench press gives more low pec development. Dumb-bell flyes can be used on a flat, incline or decline bench to vary the emphasis.

The dumb-bell pull-over is excellent for development of the deep pec line. Dips will also place great emphasis on this line if they are performed very low, that is with the shoulder below the level of the elbows. (Weights can be attached to the waist to make the dips much harder.) The use of cables, if available, is excellent for bringing out the definition at the centre of the chest (origin) due to the fact that they allow movement over the body's centre-line without loss of tension. Pectoral decks emphasise the outer part of the pecs near the insertion into the humerus (upper arm). They also relieve stress on the elbows.

If women fully develop the lower pec muscles, the result is that the bust is pushed out by large underlying muscles, thus seeming larger. Thus upper pec work and cable work enhances the cleavage.

To conclude, it has to be said that balance is the most important factor in chest development. The pecs are such a dominant muscle group visually that it is very difficult to hide faults in development. Also, all chest exercise must be balanced by back training, otherwise the chest muscles will begin to pull the shoulders round and the weaker, untrained back muscles will be unable to counteract the pull.

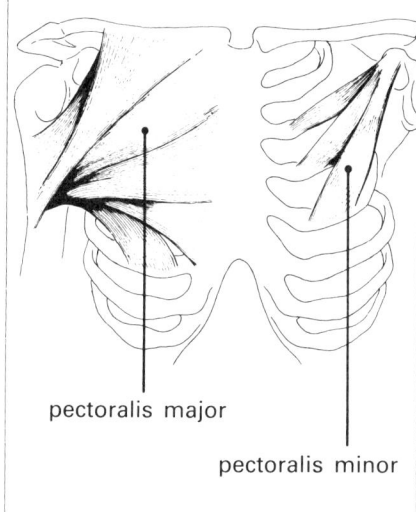

Fig. 5 Chest muscles

Back training

After the legs, the back is the most neglected area in terms of training and development. The reason for this is very simple – you can't see it. An individual will get far more pleasure working his chest, his abdominals or his arms because he can see the muscles working and developing. Also, it is much harder to train the back muscles and receive a hard pump.

The back consists of 3 main sections; the lower, the middle and the upper back. The lower back muscles, the spinal erectors, are neglected by the majority of people, and yet these muscles are perhaps the most important in the back. It is these muscles which make it possible to stand up straight and bend over to lift objects. Most back problems originate in this area, but they could be easily avoided by regular exercise of the spinal erectors. The two easiest and most basic of lower back exercises are hyperextensions and stiff-legged dead lifts. Remember to use light weights and be very cautious when first exercising the spinal erectors.

The main muscles of the middle back are the latissimus dorsi and the lower trapezius. The latissimus dorsi account for the very impressive 'V' shape of athletes and bodybuilders. These muscles draw the arms to the sides, therefore all rowing exercises, pull-ups or pull-downs are performed by them. Swimmers often have very good 'lat' development due to the fact that the arms are drawn towards the body in most styles of swimming. The lats can be exercised for width or thickness. The best exercises for developing width are wide grip pull-ups to the back of the neck and lat pull-downs. Exercises to develop thickness include seated rowing, bent-over rowing, 'T' bar rowing and single arm rowing. These latter exercises also work the lower trapezius muscles and the rhomboids.

The main muscle of the upper back is the upper trapezius. The trapezius muscle group is kite-shaped and basically pulls the head and the shoulders back. The main attachment points of these muscles to the bones are on the shoulders, the base of the skull and the middle of the back. The upper trapezius is best exercised by doing dumb-bell shrugs and upright rowing. It can also be exercised by doing shoulder presses either with dumb-bells or with barbells. It is essential to work the trapezius muscles, otherwise a stooped, round-shouldered posture will result; this is a common fault with people who do a lot of chest work but little or no back work.

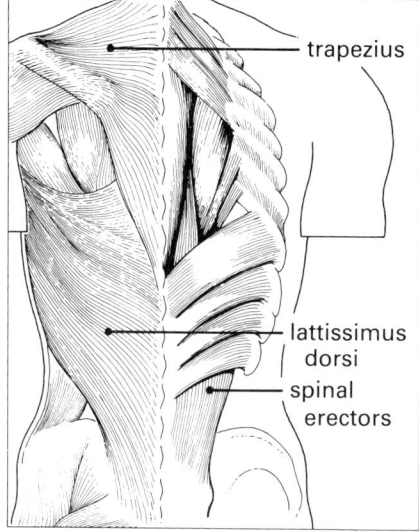

Fig. 6 Back muscles

Shoulder training

Broad shoulders are always associated with strength and are very impressive. The skeletal width of the shoulders is hereditary but an illusion of breadth can be created by fully developing the shoulder muscles. These muscles are called the deltoids and have 3 'heads'; anterior (front), lateral (side) and posterior (rear). The heads form a cap which covers the shoulder joint, and they are attached at one end to the upper arm and at the other end to 3 points to the front, top and back of the shoulder. The function of the deltoids is to raise the arm to the front, the side and the rear. All 3 of the heads of the deltoids are involved in shoulder movements, but the direction of the arm movement determines which head is being used the most.

The most impressive shoulder development shows an equal development of all 3 heads of the deltoids. However, this is not very easy to achieve. In almost all cases the anterior deltoid is the most developed and the posterior the least developed. The reason for this is very simple; the anterior deltoid is brought into play with nearly all chest exercises and is therefore always being trained more than the other heads.

The lateral and posterior heads should always be trained with specific exercises. The best exercise for the lateral deltoid is dumb-bell side-lateral raises (remember to only raise the arms to the horizontal because after this the upper trapezius will be used). The posterior deltoid is the least enjoyable to train, but should never be missed out. This head is worked hard by bent-over dumb-bell laterals or bent-over cable laterals if a cable cross-over machine is available. It is unlikely that you will need to train the anterior deltoid specifically, but if you do then the straight arm dumb-bell raises to the front are excellent.

When you start shoulder training it is best to do an exercise which works all 3 heads together and then concentrate on each head individually. The seated press behind the neck with a barbell is one of the best exercises for training the 3 heads together, but seated dumb-bell presses are also good if no barbell is available. It should be said, however, that the press behind the neck exercise works the upper trapezius quite heavily, so if the trapezius muscles are already well developed the exercise should be avoided. Alternate dumb-bell presses, which do not use the trapezius as much, could perhaps be used instead. Correctly balanced shoulder development should be aimed for if you are to avoid spoiling the whole physique.

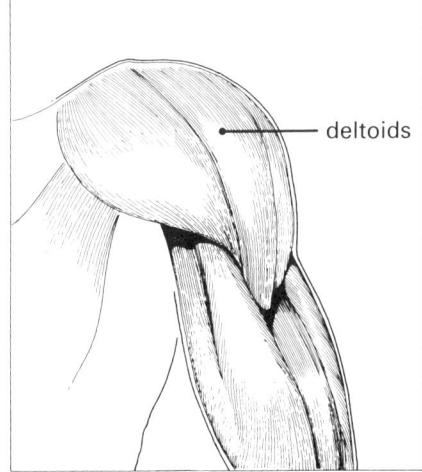

Fig. 7 Shoulder muscles

Arm training

The balance between biceps and triceps development is perhaps one of the most difficult to achieve in physique development. The triceps make up 60% of the upper arm while the biceps make up only 40% and yet it is still the case that most people tend to have overdeveloped biceps. There are two reasons for this. Firstly, training the biceps is very enjoyable and the results are easily seen. Secondly, the biceps respond very quickly to training and are relatively easy to develop compared to the triceps.

Upper arm training should be in the ratio of 3:2 for triceps to biceps. It is always best to train the triceps first because these are usually the least developed group. There are 3 heads to the triceps; 2 of them have their origins on the humerus and the third originates on the shoulder blade. The group has a single tendon insertion below the elbow into the forearm. The function of the triceps is to straighten the arm, therefore at the end of each exercise the arms should be locked out straight. If this is not done then the full range of triceps movement has not been achieved and full contraction will not be carried out, thus inhibiting development. To develop more size heavy basic exercises must be done, for example close grip bench presses, reverse grip bench presses, dips, push-downs and lying extensions. It is always advisable to have a training partner to assist when doing lying triceps exercises.

The biceps have 2 heads, the points of origin being the coracoid process on the shoulder blade and the glenoid fossa (where the humerus fits into the shallow socket of the shoulder blade). There is a single tendon insertion into the radius bone of the forearm. The function of the biceps is to bend the elbow, supinate the forearm and flex the shoulder. As with the triceps, to develop larger biceps heavy basic exercises such as barbell curls or dumb-bell curls must be performed. Dumb-bell curls should always involve rotation of the dumb-bells. This means that the biceps have been worked through their complete range of movement, aiding complete development.

Forearm training is frequently omitted because of all the work the forearms do while training other body parts. Higher repetitions must be used because the muscle type is denser and more resilient (like the calves). Wrist rolling is probably one of the best exercises to perform. This involves holding out a bar at arm's length and then rotating it. A weight can be tied to the bar by a piece of rope and then raised and lowered to make the exercise more difficult.

One final point to remember is that it is very easy to overtrain the arms. More exercises and more repetitions are not the answer to correcting poor arm development – it is better to do fewer exercises and repetitions and to take more rest.

Stretching

The benefits of stretching for people from all sports and of all ages cannot be overemphasised. However, incorrect stretching can cause untold damage and even permanent injuries in extreme cases. It is vital, therefore, that you know how to stretch properly and safely.

Some coaches believe that stretching before exercise reduces the chances of injury and helps athletic performance. But others believe that stretching should only be carried out after exercise when the muscles are warm, thus reducing the risk of tearing them. Both stretching before and stretching after exercise have their merits, but it is important to consider the type of stretching involved.

There are 2 types of stretching; static and ballistic. Static stretching involves slow, continual movement until the person is at the limit of his stretch. The pressure is then eased off and gradually reapplied to a maximum again. This is the only type of stretching which should be carried out before exercise when the muscles are cold.

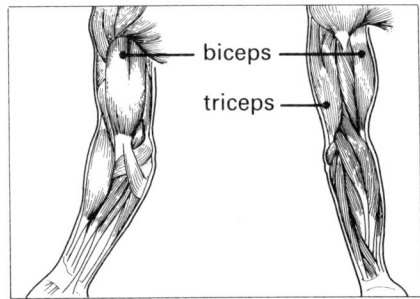

Fig. 8 Arm muscles

Ballistic stretching is more vigorous, as the name suggests, and involves bouncing and jerking movements. This type of stretching can clearly be dangerous if done before exercise when the muscles are cold, and so it should only be used at the end of a training session.

Both types of stretching increase flexibility, and as a basic rule you should do static stretching before exercise and both ballistic and static after exercise. The length of time spent stretching depends on the sport you are training for and the degree of flexibility you wish to attain.

There are now a number of stretching devices on the market. However, a machine can only stretch in a few directions and is therefore only of limited value. Most people use their own body-weight as a stretching aid, with the number of different ways to stretch being limited only by the imagination. The most important factor in 'free stretching' is that you know when it hurts and how far you can go, making it possible for you to immediately release the stretch should you need to. Safety is also an important factor when stretching with a partner; he does not know how much pain you are in and he could inadvertently overstretch you.

◀ Stretching

Aerobic activity

Aerobic activity is a form of training requiring a constant supply of oxygen to the muscles. Anaerobic activity does not require an oxygen supply to the muscles for a sudden, short burst of activity. Running is obviously an aerobic activity while weightlifting is anaerobic. To reach an aerobic state the heartbeat must be taken above 120 beats per minute and maintained above this level for twenty minutes. The benefits of this type of training for the heart and lungs are enormous, but very few people who train ever reach this level. A class which has a rest every 3 or 4 minutes but trains for an hour would be better off training non-stop for 30 minutes. This would increase the fitness of the class-members, their sense of well-being at the end of the session and also their physical appearance.

Index

abdominal board 4
adenosine triphosphate 6
adjustable bench 4
aerobic activity 31

barbell 3–4
biceps 29–30

calories 5
calves 24
carbohydrates 5–6
creatine phosphate 6

deltoids 28–9
desiccated liver 7
diet 5–8
dumb-bell 3–4

exercises 11–23
  one-arm dumb-bell rowing 20
  barbell curl 16–17
  barbell press 19
  bench press 11
  bent-over lateral raise 12
  bent-over rowing 14
  calf raise 13
  close grip bench press 22
  concentration curls 22–3
  crunches 17
  dead lift 19
  dumb-bell curls 16
  dumb-bell flyes 11
  dumb-bell shoulder press 12
  flat dumb-bell press 18
  front dumb-bell raise 18–19
  hyperextensions 14–15
  incline dumb-bell flyes 18
  knee raise 11
  leg raise 18
  lunges 13
  pull-over 11
  seated calf raise 20
  side-lateral raise 1, 11
  sit-ups 9, 11
  squats 12–13
  stiff-legged dead lift 21
  swing-bell curls 22
  triceps dips 21
  triceps extension 15
  triceps kickback 15
  twists 11
  upright rowing 14
  wrist curl 17
external oblique 25

fitness determination routine 8–10
  advanced use of 10

glutei 24–5
glycogen 6

haemoglobin 6–7

insulin 6
iron 6–7

lactic acid 6
latissimus dorsi 28
leg biceps 24–5

pectoral muscles 26–7
protein 5
pulse 8–9

quadriceps 24

rectus abdominis 25

spinal erectors 27–8
stretching 30–1
  ballistic 31
  devices 31
  'free' 31
  static 30

training
  abdominal 25–6
  arm 29–30
  back 27–8
  chest 26–7
  for size 2–3
  for speed 3
  for strength 2
  leg 24–5
  pyramid 2
  routines 23–4
  shoulder 28–9
trapezius 28–9
triceps 29–30

vitamin B 7–8
vitamin C 8

Acknowledgements
Photographs by Sandra Rowse, taken at Strands Leisure Centre, The Spiders Web Hotel, Watford – with thanks to Rebecca Evans and David Weale for demonstrating the exercises.